In the Line of Fire
A Story About D-Day

In the Line of Fire
A Story About D-Day

Tod Olson

SCHOLASTIC INC.
New York Toronto London Auckland Sydney
Mexico City New Delhi Hong Kong Buenos Aires

Cover photo
© Robert Capa/Magnum Photo

3   4   5   6   7   8   9   10   23   12   11   10   09   08   07   06   05

Contents

Introduction 6

D Minus 32 Days 9

D Minus 12 Days 13

D Minus 3 Days 19

H-Hour Minus 70 Minutes 24

H-Hour Plus 5 Minutes 28

H-Hour Plus 4 Hours 32

H-Hour Plus 10 Hours 36

D Plus 11 Weeks: Paris 40

Epilogue 45

D-Day in Photographs 46

Map: D-Day and After 52

Glossary 54

Introduction

In 1944, the world was at war, and all of America had a hated enemy—Adolf Hitler.

Hitler's Nazi Party had come to power in Germany in 1933, and it ruled with an iron fist. The Nazis believed that they belonged to a race that was better than all other races. They took everyone else's rights away.

Jews were the Nazis' main targets. They weren't allowed to vote. Their businesses were shut down or burned. And, eventually, they were sent to prison camps where they were used as slave labor—or murdered.

In 1939, the Nazi war machine began to move. Nazi tanks rolled through Poland, and World War II began. The next spring, the Nazis took control of Denmark and Norway. Then they overran Belgium, France, and Holland. By the middle of 1940, Germany controlled most of Europe.

The United States finally entered the war in December 1941. Americans joined the British and the Russians to form the Allied Forces. Together, they fought against Germany, Italy, and Japan. But the Germans still held firm in Europe.

The Allies hatched a secret plan called Operation Overlord. Allied soldiers would surprise Germany with a major attack. They would **invade** Europe and push the Germans out of the countries they'd occupied.

Early in 1944, American troops began arriving in England. Most of them were young, and few had ever fought in battle. They were just kids from places like California and New York and Kansas.

Even the officers—the men who led the troops—lacked experience. Many had been rushed through three-month training courses. They were called 90-day wonders.

By late May, there were two million Americans in England. They knew they were there to invade Europe, but they had no idea when they were leaving or where they were going. They had been told that German soldiers were fierce, and they expected the enemy to fight to the death.

D-Day, the first day of Operation Overlord, was June 6, 1944. On that day, Allied soldiers landed in German-occupied France. They were part of the largest invasion force in history—an invasion that would determine the fate of the world.

This is the story of an American soldier who took part in the D-Day invasion. His name is Keith Taber. Keith is not a real person. But his story is based on what real soldiers went through.

Follow Keith as he finds out what war is really like.

D Minus 32 Days

"Hoooo, yesss! Listen to those things fly! We're coming to get you, Hitler! Better watch your Nazi behind!"

I lifted my face off the beach and spit out some sand.

Tim was on his knees with his arms open wide and his head thrown back. His face was turned up to the sky, and tracer bullets burned the air inches above his head.

I grabbed his pack and pulled him down. He landed in a heap next to me. "Are you nuts?" I hissed. "Those are real! Do you want to live to see France, or what?"

"Relax, buddy," he said. "Those are our guys firing. Nobody gets hurt in these things."

Then I heard **Lieutenant** Mabry: "Let's go! Elbows and knees! Move it up the beach!"

I rested my forehead in the sand. The lieutenant saw me and yelled, "Taber, I know it's early, but we don't take naps during an invasion! Now crawl!"

I looked at Tim. It was 0640, or 6:40 in the morning. It was midnight when we got the order—2400. That's the way it always happened. Seven times we had done this.

Each time was practice, but it sure seemed real. We were hustled out of bed and into the landing ships. I'd have 50 pounds of gear on my back. Then there'd be waves, and I'd usually lose whatever food I'd eaten.

We'd get close to the beach. Then we'd wade out, and the firing would start. They were our guys, but they were shooting real bullets. They wanted us to know what the real thing would be like.

I pulled myself up on my elbows, and little by little I started crawling.

"I'm telling you, man, this is the worst part," Tim grunted, "all the training and waiting and stuff. It's got to be worse than the real thing."

I inched forward like a worm in the sand. A **mortar shell** blew a hole in the beach to my left, and the sand landed like rain on Tim and me. "Holy—you sure those aren't Germans up there?" I yelled.

"The Germans can't shoot that straight," he said. "Remember, bud, this is as tough as it gets."

Up ahead, a soldier stood up for a second. Then I heard him scream, and he disappeared from sight.

"**Medic**!" I heard from up ahead, and then, "Keep moving!" It was a **sergeant's** voice.

We kept crawling. In a minute or two, we saw the soldier. He was lying on his back in the sand, his left arm bleeding onto the beach. Someone had tied a bandana around his shoulder, but the blood still poured out into the sand. People just kept crawling past.

"That's a million-dollar wound," Tim said to me. "He's going home. Doesn't even know the fun he's going to miss."

I turned and lay for a second in the sand, looking back at the guy who was bleeding. His arm was almost half off, and his head was thrown back on the sand, but on his face was the faint hint of a smile.

"Move it out, Taber," barked the lieutenant. "There's no time for **rubbernecking**!" He shoved my pack, and I rolled sideways. Then I picked myself up and **slithered**, inch by inch, up the beach.

D Minus 12 Days

"Hey, Country, pound of dark chocolate says we're here another month." Jake leaned over his bunk and looked down on Tim.

"No way," Tim said. "We'll be gone in a week." Tim was from a farm in the South, and Jake grew up in New York City. They were always betting on something or challenging each other to contests. Who could eat a roast beef sandwich faster? Who could shoot a can with an M-1 from 50 yards?

Neither of them could shoot straight, though. Me, I was shooting jackrabbits from 80 yards when I was ten. Shooting Germans couldn't be that much different.

We'd all been **drafted** a few months back. None of us knew a thing about war, but we'd been through plenty of training together. Jake always called the exercises games. And the guns were toys. No matter how hard it got, it was always games and toys. "They buy expensive toys," he'd say, "and we have to use them."

Jake didn't think much of the Army. But then, he had more to miss than the rest of us. He'd gotten married just before he was drafted—Mary was her name. When he left, she was pregnant. Jake was always joking about stuff, but there was no joking about Mary. You couldn't say a thing about her.

"What do you think, Cowboy?" Jake asked me.

"I don't know," I said, "but I know I'm sick of waiting."

"You've got to admit, though, the food's great," said Tim. "Steak last night—all you can eat—and then ice cream. I ate like a pig."

"That's exactly what the Army thinks you are," said Jake. "They're fattening you up for the kill."

We all laughed. Then Tim replied, "The only

pigs dying this month will be German ones. It'll be sausages for dinner in Paris, baby!"

We'd been in England for three months now, and we all knew why—the Germans had taken over the rest of Europe.

There were all these little villages. People there were just minding their own business—then the Nazis came in with tanks and heavy guns. They just ran right over everyone, and now they were making them live under German laws.

What if they didn't stop there? Next thing you know, we'd have German tanks rolling through Idaho. At least, that's what the Army said. I didn't know if it was true, but it had a lot of us scared. We had to go to France and get the Germans out.

But before we went, the Army had to teach us how to do it, so we attacked empty beaches. They were nice places, too. They probably used to be full of nice British guys getting sunburns with their girlfriends.

But now the beaches were full of holes. We'd blown up one empty beach after another. I couldn't believe all the bullets we'd buried in the sand.

Now that all the training was over, we just waited. We slept in tents near the water. Someone said there were two million guys— English, Americans, Canadians. We all knew we were going to France, but nobody knew exactly when or where.

Parking lots full of tanks just sat there, all of them covered by nets. The nets were painted to look like the ground, so when German planes buzzed over, they wouldn't see a thing.

We had to stay in our camp at all times. A few guys snuck out to a bar once. When they got caught, they were stuck on kitchen duty for a week.

Everyone was going crazy waiting. There were fights every night, and yesterday some nut threw a clip of M-1 shells into a burning barrel. It sounded like the Fourth of July.

Sometimes I went down to the English Channel and just looked out over the water. We had a few miles of water to cross to get to France and all those Germans. Sometimes it seemed like you could spit on their heads from here, and sometimes it seemed like they were a world away.

"Have you ever met a German?" I asked.

Tim and a couple of other guys said no.

"See what I mean?" said Jake. "We're supposed to kill these guys, but who knows what they're even like?"

Two bunks over, a guy named Gabe spoke up: "Ever met anyone from 3 Troop?"

"Nope."

"Those guys are all Jews from Europe, and they hate the Nazis. They say Hitler's just wiping out all the Jews he can find. I spoke to one of them who said he'd never thought of himself as a Jew. He was even in the Hitler Youth, training to become a good Nazi.

"But the Nazis found out that his great-grandfather was a Jew, so they kicked him out of the Hitler Youth. Then his mom and dad disappeared, and some uncle or something helped him sneak out of the country."

"What happened to his folks?"

"He doesn't know, but he figures that they're dead."

"Just because one of them had a Jewish grandfather?"

"I guess."

The tent got quiet. I dreamt that night that the Germans just gave up—that it really was just a game. We bombed the right number of empty beaches, and they had to **surrender**.

D Minus 3 Days

The model was perfect. They must have spent weeks making it. It was just sand and wood and clay, but it looked like a real beach. There were little tank barriers and little machine gun nests. There were even little **bunkers** up on the hill. It was supposed to look like the beach we were invading.

The whole thing sat on a table in the **briefing** tent, and we all stood around it like a bunch of shepherds looking at baby Jesus.

The **colonel** gave us the plan. It seemed so easy. At least that's the way he made it sound.

We'd be waiting off the coast by dawn, he'd said. At **H-Hour** minus 70 minutes, our planes would appear, dropping bombs like hail on the Germans.

The battleships would start firing, shells

would rake the beach, and then we'd land.

By that time, the Nazis would either be dead or driven out. We'd blow up the barriers and move up the roads with tanks and heavy guns.

Then we'd find our way to Paris, and after that, Berlin—the capital of Germany itself. They had it all figured out.

"The world is watching you, men," the colonel had said. "Millions of lives depend on your work. French ladies want the Nazis out of their homes, Europe wants its freedom back, and three million American boys want to go home to their families."

I felt a nudge. Jake was standing next to me at the model. "That colonel can't read a map," he whispered. "The way home is over the Atlantic Ocean—not across the English Channel."

Tim leaned across me toward Jake. "I'm not leaving without Hitler's head," he said. "If we do, he'll be knocking on *our* doors in a year."

I looked at the miniature beach. The real one was supposed to be 300 yards deep at low tide, with steep hills and cliffs along the back.

On top of the cliffs were German bunkers. They were big square things, each one made of thick concrete. Inside were huge guns—155s, 88s, **grenade** launchers, you name it. They just sat there, pointing at the beach.

I started thinking the colonel was crazy. Anyone on the beach would be a sitting duck. The only place to take cover was a long, low wall of rocks halfway up the beach. If you made it there, you'd be safe—but only for a while.

"Suppose the Air Force guys don't take out those bunkers," I said.

"Then we're going to get chewed up," said Jake. "That's what I've been telling you. A guy in the 116th said we're cannon food. Nine out of ten won't make it."

"Geez, I'm sorry about that," Tim said. "I'm going to miss you guys."

I laughed, but it was a weak sound, and it

died away fast. In a minute, we went outside and walked back to the tent. Nobody spoke.

Suddenly, a shot cracked the silence. A crowd was gathering up ahead. We pushed our way in.

Over a shoulder, I saw a guy on the ground, his rifle lying next to him. His hands gripped his left calf as blood poured from the boot beneath it. Pain squeezed his face into wrinkles, but his eyes looked bright. You just knew he had done it on purpose. He was going home.

"You bloody coward!" said a voice in the crowd.

"Bloody smart is what he is," Jake replied. "He knows the way home."

We pushed our way out of the crowd and walked back to our tent in silence. The lights went out at 2200.

"Hey, Taber," Tim whispered.

"Yeah?"

"You think we're going to make it, right?"

I didn't know what to say. I just grunted.

"Well, I'm getting out of my stupid town when I get home," he said. "I'm moving to New York City. I'll work construction, hang out with Jake, maybe even get married. Our kids could play together. You should come too, man."

"Yeah," I said, "maybe when it's all over."

I rolled over. Tim didn't say anything more. In a minute, I reached for my rifle. Its weight trapped my hand against the bed, and my palm felt sweaty on the grip. I tried to imagine pulling the trigger.

It would only take one shot, I thought. In a month I'd be walking again—and I'd be home. I'd be taking my little sister to the fair, and I'd be alive. What would it matter? There were two million more just like me. Let them be heroes.

I couldn't do it. It's not like I wanted to be a hero. But I didn't want to be a coward, either.

H-Hour Minus 70 Minutes

I gripped the side of the boat in the darkness, every new wave almost knocking me over. It was as if the sea itself was trying to throw me out of the boat.

For five hours, I'd been fighting the lump in my stomach. I'd feel it rise and then drop again—over and over. All I wanted was to get sick. I felt it rise again. I pressed my hand to my mouth, but it just kept rising. I leaned toward the side of the boat. A wave jolted me back in—and that's when it all came out.

I opened my eyes and saw my vomit floating in seawater at the bottom of the boat. It sloshed against Tim's legs. I looked up, expecting some **wisecrack**, but Tim was holding the side of the boat like a wild horse's reins. His eyes were pinched shut.

I looked around at our unit. We were

supposed to be cool, well-trained fighting machines, but Jake was bent over the side of the boat, trying to puke into the ocean, and Gabe had been knocked over by the weight of his pack. He wasn't even trying to get up.

Then there was Tim. His eyes were shut so tight it probably hurt. It made me think of my little sister. She used to close her eyes and say she was hiding. She was right there in plain sight, but she couldn't see the rest of the world, so she thought the world couldn't see her either.

When we'd boarded the boats, it hadn't been so terrifying. And there were so many of them. I didn't know that many could even fit in the ocean. They were lined up side by side along the coast, so close you could almost step from the deck of one boat to the next. I bet you could have walked from one end of England to the other on those boats.

Another wave rocked the boat, and I felt the lump rise again. I looked out into the darkness, knowing that somewhere out there was a beach. I didn't care how many machine guns were there. I just wanted to be off the boat. In my mind, I knew two things: Bullets could kill you, and seasickness could not. But it didn't matter. I'd take my chances with the bullets.

I was ready to puke again. Just then, the sky brightened in the east. The outline of a beach came into view, and you could hear the buzz of a thousand planes in the air. In seconds, the beach was lit by explosions, and towers of fire burst from the sand.

A cheer rose from the boat, and I could hear Tim yell above the noise. "Get 'em, boys," he screamed, pumping his fist in the air. I could see landing boats scattered across the water, each one full of men staring at the beach. Twenty yards away there was another landing boat, and for a second I caught the eye of a kid in it. He looked about 12, I swear. He must have lied about his age. He wasn't even watching the bombs. He just looked plain scared.

For maybe 15 minutes, our **bombers** did their work. Fire just rained from the sky. It was like every star fell and exploded on the ground. I imagined the German bunkers getting blown into big piles of dust.

Tim turned to me and yelled, "Didn't I tell you? It's going to be a piece of cake!" Just then, I heard a familiar whining sound as an explosion ripped through the water 100 yards away. Everyone in the boat ducked, and in a minute, the air was full of German shells. They were coming from the cliffs behind the beach.

They're shooting at me, I thought—at *me*—and this isn't practice. They want to *kill* me. I **crouched** down, leaning against the side of the boat. I knew it wouldn't protect me, but for some reason it made me feel safe. I let my head pop up, and there was that kid in the next boat again. Now he looked even younger than 12. He was crouching, too. Just his head stuck up over the side, and I could see that his eyes were shut tight. I think he thought he was hiding—like Tim, like my little sister.

Then he was gone. There was that terrible whine—and then the blast. A shell hit the kid's boat dead center, and a spout of water shot from the ocean.

H-Hour Plus 5 Minutes

"You're not dropping us here!" Lieutenant Mabry was right in the Navy captain's face. "My men will drown!"

Shells were still screaming all around us. "I can't get this ship blown up," the captain said. "I've got more guys to bring in."

To our right, a landing ship was unloading 500 yards from the beach. The ramp was down, and men were walking into the waves. Then they would disappear in maybe 10 feet of water. The lucky ones got rid of their packs. They dropped their guns and everything else so they could swim. The unlucky ones just didn't come up.

The lieutenant was bursting with anger. In a second he had a pistol in his hand. He pointed it at the captain's head. "I said take us in!" he shouted.

The captain stared at the gun. Then he started moving the boat in closer.

In a few minutes, we were 150 yards from shore. The captain looked at the lieutenant. "I'm dropping the ramp!" he said. Lieutenant Mabry didn't answer. He just stared at the captain.

Finally, he turned to us and said, "Let's go!" That was it—just, "Let's go!" There was no big speech like you see in the movies. We just turned and walked into the water. Tim and Jake were in front of me, and I watched them both go under. Seconds later, they popped up without their packs. I couldn't believe it. We were like those animals that follow each other off cliffs. They know they're going to die, but they do it anyway.

I think the lieutenant was the first to get hit. After that, I don't know—bullets just raked the water around us. I know it's weird, but the bullets looked like water from a garden hose, and I kept thinking about my mom. I could see her standing in her garden, watering the tomatoes.

I kept wading. I waded through potatoes and squash and peas. I waded through pole beans and carrots. And I didn't think about the bodies until I was on the beach. The water was littered with them, many face down like they were looking for fish.

But Gabe was face up.

His eyes were open, staring at the sky. The water was blackish red around him, and I counted three holes in his shirt. I brushed him away like a corn stalk, and two more bullets hit him. The force pushed him back toward me, and I pushed him away again.

I hit the beach and ran. At least I thought I was running, but I wasn't moving any faster than the guy next to me. He was limping up the beach, and blood was pouring from his leg. All around us, bullets hit the sand. They made little noises—*sip, sip*—like someone sucking air through their teeth.

I don't know how long it took. It seemed like hours, even though I think it was more like five minutes. But, finally, I made it to the wall of rocks. I lay against it and looked out at the

Channel. Everywhere, guys were running in slow motion up the beach. Every few seconds, someone would go down. It looked like they'd just tripped, but they wouldn't get up.

I shut my eyes tight. I imagined my sister curled up in a chair with her hands over her eyes—hiding. I sat that way for a while. I couldn't see them; they couldn't see me. I almost shut it all out—the blast of the mortars, the *sip, sip* of the bullets.

And then the sound of weeping slipped through. Again, I pictured my sister. It wasn't a loud bawling, like the sound she makes when she wants everyone to hear her. It was more like the quiet, desperate sound she makes when some terrible nightmare wakes her up on a peaceful night.

I opened my eyes and looked to my left. It was Tim. He was sitting with his knees drawn up to his chest. His helmet was off, and he was sobbing like he'd never stop.

H-Hour Plus 4 Hours

We were still sitting behind the wall when this colonel walked by. I can't remember what he said. He was crazy though. He was walking along the wall. The machine gunners could see him clear as day, but he didn't care. He just **strutted** along, yelling at us.

"You can die here, or you can die killing Germans." It was something like that. It seemed like a funny way to get us moving. I mean, dying is dying. What do you care what you're doing when it happens?

But he was right about one thing: We were going to die if we sat there. The machine guns couldn't see us, but the mortar guys were zeroing in. Their shells were dropping closer all the time. They left big holes in the sand when they hit.

The mortars turned men into rag dolls. One

second, a guy would be running. Then you'd hear that whine, and fear would hit his face for a moment. Then the sand would explode, and he'd be lifeless on the beach.

It was weird to think how quickly it happened. You work so hard to get to be 17. I mean, you worry yourself sick about homework and girlfriends and making the baseball team— and then it's all over in a second.

I turned to Tim. He'd barely moved in a couple of hours.

"Hey, man," I said, "you okay?"

He didn't say anything.

"Tim, come on! You've got to pull it together. We can't stay here."

He whimpered something through his hands. "What?" I said.

"He was carrying his arm," Tim was shaking his head slowly.

"Carrying *what*?" I asked.

"His arm. I saw him from behind. I thought it was a rifle at first, but there was blood everywhere."

"Oh, man, you can't think about it, Tim. We

have to get out of here."

"I got up there and it was Jake. He just kept saying, 'I won't drop it. I won't drop it.'"

I didn't know what to say.

Tim was talking through sobs now. "I just ran by. I turned my head so he wouldn't see it was me, and I ran by. . . ."

He sat up like he'd just realized he'd forgotten something important. "Oh, my God! I have to find him."

Tim stood up straight and started to look around. Machine gun fire tore at the top of the ridge next to him, but he barely noticed. I reached for his sleeve and pulled him back down.

He collapsed in a heap next to me, and we just lay there, leaning on each other.

I guess an hour passed. I don't know. Everything around me sounded like a bad radio station. You know, like the sound was coming in and out. I would hear things, and then the blast from a shell would break it all up.

I remember a sergeant saying our group was nearly gone. Only six of us were still alive— out of 30. Then there was a blast. I remember

Tim saying something about Jake—then another blast—and then he was talking about his mother. I could hardly understand anything he was saying.

Just then, a shell blew up near us. It must have been an 88. It landed 20 yards to our right, and a boot with a foot still in it dropped near my hand.

Right then, a sergeant came running down the line. "Come on!" he was yelling. "I'm not dying on this beach. Let's get us some Germans!"

He went right over the wall. He was charging at the hills, and people started following. In a second, Tim was up and moving. Anger was in his face like a fever. I didn't really feel mad at anyone—not the Germans, not that colonel, not the sergeant—I was just plain scared.

H-Hour Plus 10 Hours

It was weird. You could see the machine gun. It was spitting bullets through a hole in a concrete wall. But you couldn't see a person. I felt like it was just a big piece of metal we were after—like there was no flesh involved, nothing breathing or beating.

The gun sat right over a road. It was the main exit from the beach. There were big tank barriers on the road. Our guys were trying to blow them up, but they were just getting mowed down by this gun.

We had gone around the road. We went up a grassy hill where the guns couldn't get us, but the Germans had buried **mines** everywhere. The worst were the Bouncing Betties. If you stepped on one, it shot up from the ground. Then it went off at waist height, sending metal into you like a hundred knives.

I was walking on my toes. It was stupid, I know, but I thought that way if I hit one it wouldn't go off.

We made it off the beach. We were 100 feet up, and I suddenly noticed something really weird: I could hear mortars and machine guns, but none of them were shooting at us. They were all pointed at the beach—we were *behind* them!

For ten hours, I'd been ducking. Every blast had made me think how soft I was. I don't mean weak, really, just soft, temporary. It was my body against a whole lot of dumb metal, and I didn't stand a chance. But now I was safe—for a while.

I looked at Tim. He was crouched next to me in the bushes. He was staring at the machine gun bunker, but his eyes didn't seem to be focused on anything.

"How are you doing?" I asked.

"They shot his arm off!" he said, his eyes like steel.

"Maybe he made it anyway. You don't know." But Tim wasn't listening.

The sergeant crawled over. It was the guy who had led us up the ridge. He whispered to Tim: "Private, let's move out. You take the left. I've got the right." Then he turned to me: "Son, you shoot at any head that pops up."

The two of them started creeping toward the bunker, and the machine gun spit out another round of bullets. Tim and the sergeant moved closer. Then they split up, and I lost sight of the sergeant. Tim moved carefully around the left side of the bunker and pulled a grenade from his belt. He pulled out the pin and stuffed the grenade through a tiny slit in the concrete wall.

The bunker muffled the blast, but I knew it was big. I saw a German soldier stumble out. He was hurt pretty badly. Tim pulled out his pistol, pointed it at the soldier's head, and shot. The guy's head jerked back, and he crumpled to the ground. Then Tim gave out a kind of yell, lifted his rifle, and brought the butt down hard on the guy's head.

He was still doing that when I saw another German come out of the bushes. It happened so fast I can barely remember. All I know is this:

He was raising his arm as he walked toward Tim, so I leveled my M-1, sighted, and put five rounds in his chest.

Tim stopped when he heard the shots and crouched down like an animal. I waited a couple of minutes. Then I headed for the bunker. The sergeant and Tim were standing over the guy I shot.

"Good shot, kid," said the sergeant.

I didn't answer. The body was lying still, its arms and legs spread out in all directions. It was like death had pulled them off and a blind person had put them all back.

His face was white and scared and young. He looked like the kid on the landing boat, the one I had watched get blown up.

The sergeant and Tim walked to the edge of the cliff. I took one last look at the kid's body, and then I joined them. The machine gun was silent now. Down below, our guys were busy. They'd blown a big hole in the concrete, and a tank was crawling through.

Behind us, the sunset was rusting the sky. Tim stood next to me. His face was blank.

D Plus 11 Weeks: Paris

We rode in like movie stars or something. Paris was the capital of France. The Nazis had been there for four years, and the French hated them. Now the Nazis were gone, and we had chased them out, so the French *loved* us.

We rode in tanks and trucks and jeeps. I couldn't believe the crowds. Up and down the streets, people were cheering. Girls were coming up and kissing us—just like that. They wouldn't even tell you their names. They'd just hug you and kiss you. Then they'd say "thank you" in that cute French accent.

Tim rode next to me on the truck. He just sat and took it all in. He didn't say much anymore—not since the beach. I was pretty quiet, too. I just didn't have much to say. Next to bullets, words didn't seem all that important.

The days were okay. We were on the move,

and there wasn't much to do. The Germans were on the run. We still had to watch out for mines, and there were **snipers** in the trees, but there wasn't that much danger.

The nights were the worst. Falling asleep was like trying to enter a heavily guarded room. I'd get halfway in the door, but then I'd hear a blast in my dreams—like mortars or grenades—and I'd be wide awake again. Then I'd start all over. We didn't talk about it, but I know it was the same for Tim.

We never doubted that we were fighting on the right side though. The French people would tell us stories about the Nazis. In one place, the Nazis found a radio. Some French guys had been calling in information to the British, so the Nazis took them to the town square and shot them, right there in the open.

One woman hadn't seen her husband or her two sons in months. They'd been taken away to work in a factory somewhere, and she hadn't heard a thing.

Another village lost about 40 Jews. They were sent to prison camps by the Nazis. No one knew if they were still alive.

"Taber?" Tim was looking out the side of the truck.

"Yeah?"

"What are you going to tell them all?"

"Who?" I asked.

"People back home—your parents, friends."

"I don't know," I said.

All the images came back to me: Gabe floating in the water, Tim sobbing into his hands, the kid I shot. Why couldn't he have just surrendered? A lot of the German guys were thrilled to surrender. Some of them would throw down their guns and hug you. They'd have these great big smiles on their faces. Why didn't this guy just do that?

I looked out into the crowd. Right in front, there was a tall guy with a little girl on his shoulders. She had blonde hair and pigtails, and her blue dress looked like the Montana sky. Her chin rested on the man's head, and she was playing peekaboo with the guys on the tanks.

I leaned out of the truck to watch her. In a minute, she disappeared into the crowd.

I turned to Tim. "I don't think I'll tell them much," I said.

Tim looked at me and nodded. The truck banged on through Paris. That girl was probably still back there. I could just see her, perched up high. Her arms were out like she was welcoming the world, and she was beaming like she'd never heard of war.

Epilogue

It was August of 1944 when the Allies rolled into Paris. Eight months later, the war in Europe was over. Adolf Hitler killed himself in an underground bunker.

Many American soldiers stayed in Europe after the war. They helped the Europeans rebuild. It was no easy task. Thirty to forty million Europeans had died, and entire cities had been destroyed by bombs.

Most American soldiers simply went home. Some got married and had kids. Others got money from the government to go to college. Most of them were changed forever by the war. Many had seen men die. Some had killed with their own hands. But nearly everyone felt that one thing was true: Hitler had put the world in extreme danger, and they had found the courage to do the right thing.

D-Day in Photographs

D-Day was the first day of Operation Overlord, the largest military invasion in history.

D-Day was June 6, 1944. About 150,000 Allied soldiers, 5,000 ships, and 11,000 aircraft were involved. They were invading the beaches of Normandy, on the coast of France.

At dawn, Capa's landing ship approached Omaha Beach.

D-Day was a top-secret operation, so not many photographs were taken.

Robert Capa was one of the few photographers there. Early in the morning of June 6, he got on a ship loaded with soldiers. They were headed for Omaha Beach in Normandy. Here's some of what Capa saw.

National Archives, Still Pictures Branch

Soldiers dragged themselves to shore. This one moved past barricades Germans had placed in the water to block ships.

At Omaha Beach, the landing ships couldn't get all the way to the shore, so soldiers had to jump out and wade. Notice the beach and cliffs of Normandy in the background.

Omaha was one of five beaches the Allies invaded on D-Day. The soldiers at Omaha were under very heavy fire.

The Allies took over Omaha Beach, but the losses were heavy. About 3,000 Allied soldiers were killed there.

After the battle, the Allied soldiers moved inland. They planned to free France, and all of Europe, from the Germans.

© Robert Capa/Magnum Photo

Eleven weeks after D-Day, the troops arrived in Paris, the capital of France. There, the people welcomed them wildly.

D-Day and After

ENGLAND

HOLLAND

ALLIED LANDINGS

Antwerp
BELGIUM
Brussels

ENGLISH CHANNEL°

Bastogne

Brest

Caen

BR. 2ND ARMY

Battle
of the Bulge

LUX.

U.S. 1ST ARMY

Rhine River

Paris

Le Mans

St. Nazaire

Nantes

U.S. 3RD ARMY

Orléans

Dijon

BAY OF
BISCAY

FRANCE

SWITZERL

U.S. 7TH ARMY

FR. 1ST ARMY

Lyon

ITAL

Allied Nations

Axis Powers

Countries occupied by
Axis Powers prior to D-Day

Neutral countries

Front line and breakout
July 24

Front line Sept. 15

N

Marseilles

MEDITERRAN
SEA

SPAIN

0   50   100
MILES

ALLIED LANDINGS

This map shows where Allied troops landed on D-Day. It also shows their progress across Europe.

At the time, most of Europe was held by the Axis powers—Germany and its supporters.

The Allies' plan was to land in France and take countries back from the Axis.

At the top left of the map, you can see where the Allies landed on D-Day, June 6, 1944.

There, the Allies faced hard fighting. Finally, on July 24, they broke through. Then they moved across France.

On August 25, Allied armies reached Paris, France's capital.

On September 15, the Allied troops crossed into Germany. The dotted line shows how far the armies had come.

But in December, the Germans struck back. At the Battle of the Bulge, the Allies fought the tough German soldiers in bitter cold.

In January, the Allies managed to win this battle. And on May 7, 1945, Germany surrendered.

Jim McMahon

Glossary

bombers *(noun)* planes that drop bombs

briefing *(adjective)* having to do with a meeting that is held to share information

bunkers *(noun)* strong forts or shelters

colonel *(noun)* an officer in the Army, lower than a general

crouched *(verb)* bent down *(related words: crouch, crouching)*

D-Day *(noun)* the date that a secret attack is going to happen

drafted *(verb)* forced to serve in the army, usually to help fight a war

grenade *(noun)* a small bomb that is thrown by hand or fired from a rifle

H-Hour *(noun)* the exact time that a secret attack is going to start

invade *(verb)* to send soldiers into another country; to attack *(related words: invaded, invading, invasion)*

lieutenant *(noun)* an officer in the Army, lower than a colonel

medic *(noun)* someone who helps soldiers who are hurt during a battle *(related words: medical, medicine)*

mines *(noun)* bombs that are placed underground or underwater

mortar *(noun)* a very short cannon that fires shells or rockets

rubbernecking *(verb)* stopping to stare at something

sergeant *(noun)* an officer in the Army, lower than a lieutenant

shell *(noun)* the case around a bullet or a type of small bomb

slithered *(verb)* moved along the ground like a snake *(related words: slither, slithering)*

snipers *(noun)* people who shoot at others from hidden places

strutted *(verb)* walked in a proud or confident way *(related words: strut, strutting)*

surrender *(verb)* to give up *(related words: surrendered, surrendering)*

wisecrack *(noun)* a funny remark or joke